curry

curry

easy recipes for all your favourites

Sunil Vijayakar

photography by Kate Whitaker

RYLAND
PETERS
& SMALL

LONDON NEW YORK

Dedication
For Geraldine and Finn, with love.

Design and photographic art direction
Steve Painter
Senior Commissioning Editor Julia Charles
Senior Editor Céline Hughes
Production Controller Toby Marshall
Art Director Leslie Harrington
Publishing Director Alison Starling

Food Stylist Sunil Vijayakar
Prop Stylist Penny Markham
Indexer Sandra Shotter

Author's acknowledgements
Thanks to Steve for his fabulous art direction, to
Céline for her meticulous and amazing editing, to
Julia for commissioning me, to Kate for her terrific
photography, and to Belinda for assisting me.

First published in the United Kingdom
in 2008 by Ryland Peters & Small
20–21 Jockey's Fields
London WC1R 4BW
www.rylandpeters.com

10 9 8 7 6 5 4 3 2 1

ISBN: 978 1 84597 729 0

A CIP record for this book is available from the
British Library.

Printed in China

Notes
• All spoon measurements are level, unless otherwise
specified.

• Ovens should be preheated to the specified
temperature. Recipes in this book were tested using
a regular oven. If using a fan-assisted oven, follow
the manufacturer's instructions for adjusting
temperatures.

• All eggs are medium, unless otherwise specified.
Recipes containing raw or partially cooked egg, or
raw fish or shellfish, should not be served to the very
young, very old, anyone with a compromised
immune system or pregnant women.

• Sterilize preserving jars before use. Wash them in
hot, soapy water and rinse in boiling water. Place in
a large saucepan and then cover with hot water.
With the lid on, bring the water to the boil and
continue boiling for 15 minutes. Turn off the heat,
then leave the jars in the hot water until just before
they are to be filled. Invert the jars onto clean
kitchen paper to dry. Sterilize the lids for 5 minutes,
by boiling, or according to the manufacturer's
instructions. Jars should be filled and sealed while
they are still hot.

contents

introduction

The word 'curry' is believed to originate from the south Indian Tamil word 'kari', which generally describes a stew-like dish seasoned with aromatic spices and herbs. As we become increasingly global in our appreciation of food, we now know and embrace curries from all around the world, but mainly India, Pakistan, Thailand, Sri Lanka, Indonesia, Vietnam, Burma and other Southeast Asian countries. Curries differ greatly in taste, content, texture and flavour, each with vast regional variations and history.

Living in the West, especially in the bigger cities, we are fortunate to have such a wide variety of restaurants and eateries, due to pockets of immigrant communities that have settled here, offering authentic cuisines. There is nothing more satisfying, though, than cooking a great curry from scratch in the comfort of your own kitchen. The idea may seem daunting to the novice cook or to someone who is unfamiliar with the cuisine, but you will soon realize that cooking curries is easy, relaxing and rewarding.

You will need a well-stocked storecupboard of basic ingredients and spices. Most of these can be found in any large supermarkets or greengrocers and with the miracle of internet shopping, you can source any exotic ingredients and have them delivered to your door (see websites & mail order, page 94). You do not need any special equipment to start cooking, just frying pans or a wok, saucepans and a food processor. Armed with your treasure trove of ingredients and spices, go ahead and enjoy cooking up the various different curries for your friends and family.

The essence of cooking curries lies in the quality of the ingredients you use, and in particular the wonderful combinations of spices, aromatics, herbs and other flavourings that are blended and cooked to produce aromatic flavours and tastes. I urge you to browse the shelves of Asian supermarkets and greengrocers to inspire your culinary zeal and nurture your taste for the exotic. The smell of warm spices permeating the air and the piles of glorious, healthy fresh produce will be enough to have you wanting to get into your kitchen and start cooking!

ingredients

spices

Amchoor Also known as mango powder, this pale yellow powder made from dried unripe mango has a tart, fruity tang with a hint of sweetness. If unavailable, use a dash of lime or lemon juice, or tamarind water instead.

Cardamom This sweetly aromatic spice with a gingery, musky fragrance is used in sweet and savoury dishes. The pods can be added to rice or split open and the seeds ground or used whole. The ground seeds are used in spice mixes such as garam masala.

Cassia Also known as Chinese cinnamon, cassia has a coarser appearance than cinnamon and a stronger flavour. If cassia is unavailable, use cinnamon instead.

Chillies Whole dried red chillies can be fiery, so use with caution. They are usually fried to enhance and intensify their flavour. Dried chilli flakes are also available and tend to be slightly milder. Chilli powders made from dried chillies are usually labelled hot, medium or mild. Kashmiri chilli powder, made from dried red Kashmiri chillies, is fiery-hot, while paprika is extremely mild, slightly sweet and smoky.

Cinnamon This sweet, warming spice is used to flavour sweet and savoury dishes. It comes from the bark of a tree related to the laurel family and is available whole or ground. Cinnamon sticks should be discarded from a dish before serving.

Cloves These very dark brown buds of an evergreen tree are pungent so they are used (whole or ground) in small quantities. Whole cloves should be discarded before serving.

Coriander The beige seeds of the coriander plant have a warm, burnt-orange aroma and are used whole or ground. To grind the seeds yourself, toast them first in a dry frying pan to release the flavour.

Cumin These small, long beige seeds are used whole or ground. They have a distinctive warm, pungent aroma and are usually fried first to intensify their flavour. Whole seeds may be toasted and sprinkled over a dish before serving. To grind the seeds yourself, toast them first in a dry frying pan to release the flavour.

Curry leaves These small, dark green leaves have a distinctive curry-like aroma and are found fresh in Asian stores. They freeze well. Dried leaves are not as aromatic as fresh leaves. Fresh curry leaves are usually fried first to release their flavour.

Curry powders & pastes Ready-made curry powders and pastes are an invention of the West, but are nonetheless useful cupboard staples. There are many varieties, usually mild, medium or hot, as well as specific mixes such as Madras curry powder, or tandoori spice mix. You can also get very good Thai green and red curry pastes.

Fennel These small, pale greenish-brown seeds have a subtle aniseed flavour. They are used as a flavouring or served after the meal as a digestive and breath freshener.

Fenugreek Mainly used in north Indian cooking, these tiny, yellowish seeds are used in pickles, chutneys and vegetarian dishes.

Garam masala Every household has its own variation of this classic spice mix, which is usually added towards the end of cooking time. A classic mix contains cardamom, cloves, peppercorns, cumin, cinnamon and nutmeg. Ready-made mixes can be bought from supermarkets and Asian stores.

Mustard seeds These are an essential flavouring in Indian cooking, particularly dals, vegetarian and rice dishes, and pickles. Black, brown and yellow mustard seeds are usually fried until they pop to achieve a mellow, nutty flavour. The crushed, whole seeds are very peppery and are sometimes added to pickles.

Nigella Also known as black onion seeds or kalonji, these tiny, pungent black seeds are often used to flavour breads and pickles.

Peppercorns Native to the Malabar coast, these tiny, pungent berries are a very popular flavouring. They may be used whole, crushed or freshly ground. Avoid the ready-ground spice, because it loses the fresh, pungent bite of the whole spice.

Saffron Harvested from a special crocus, these deep orange strands are used to impart a wonderfully musky fragrance to rice dishes and desserts. It is one of the most expensive spices, but only a little is needed, and it is well worth the cost. Avoid the powdered spice which is not as flavourful and may have been adulterated.

Tamarind Used as a souring agent to bring out and enhance the flavour of other ingredients, tamarind has a sharp, fruity tang. It is obtained from a pod and is usually available as a pulp, paste or purée. The pulp needs to be soaked in hot water for several hours, then strained; the paste or purée can be dissolved in hot water.

Turmeric This bright orange-yellow rhizome has a warm, musky flavour and is used in small quantities in vegetable and lentil dishes. The fresh spice can sometimes be found in Asian stores, but it is usually easier to buy the dried, ground spice.

Urad dal A type of lentil, urad dal is used as a spice in south Indian cooking – fried first to release and intensify its nutty flavour.

wet spices & aromatics

Chillies Fresh green and red chillies are used to give heat and flavour to many curry dishes, although it should be noted that not all curries contain chillies, and many curries can be mild. Green chillies are more commonly used, although the riper red chillies feature in many dishes. Much of the heat resides in the seeds and pith so unless you want a fiery-hot dish, remove the seeds and pith before chopping the flesh.

Garlic Garlic is used with ginger and onion as the base of many classic curries. There is no substitute for the flavour of fresh garlic, which is usually sliced, crushed or grated and fried before other spices are added.

Ginger Fresh root ginger is another essential aromatic, used in savoury and sweet dishes. It has a fresh, zesty, peppery flavour; dried ground ginger is no substitute. Look for ginger with a smooth, light brown skin and peel before slicing, dicing or grating.

Onions Onion is usually classed as a vegetable but it is such an essential flavouring (frequently used with garlic and fresh ginger), that it deserves to be placed among wet spices and aromatics.

Shallots These small, pungent members of the onion family are used in the same way as onions, and are used particularly in south Indian and south Asian cooking.

herbs

Bay leaves The whole leaves are used only occasionally in curries; the dried, ground leaves are sometimes used in garam masala.

Coriander Fresh coriander is an important ingredient in many savoury dishes, salads and chutneys. Its delicate leaves have a distinctive, fragrant aroma, and are usually added to dishes just before serving.

Kaffir lime leaves Highly aromatic leaves from the kaffir lime tree, usually used finely shredded or left whole. The fresh leaves freeze very well and are superior to dried.

Lemongrass This citrus-flavoured 'grass' is used whole by bruising the base to release the flavour, or it can be finely chopped.

Mint Fresh, zesty mint is popular in many dishes and chutneys. Although dried mint is widely available, it does not have the same zest as the fresh herb.

Thai sweet basil leaves These fragrant leaves are used to garnish many Thai and Southeast Asian-style curries.

cupboard staples

Coconut Another essential ingredient, coconut milk and cream are added to savoury dishes to add a rich sweetness and smooth, creamy texture. Although you can make your own coconut milk from fresh coconuts, it is much easier to use the tinned variety, of which there are healthier low-fat versions. Desiccated coconut is also commonly used.

Gram flour Also known as besan, this golden flour made from ground chickpeas has a lovely, slightly nutty flavour and is used for thickening, binding and making batters.

Nuts & seeds These play an important role in the Indian kitchen. Ground almonds and cashew nuts are a popular addition to savoury dishes, while pistachio nuts are often used to garnish savoury dishes and desserts. Poppy seeds are usually toasted to intensify their taste, and used to flavour curries. White poppy seeds (khus khus) are mainly used to thicken curries.

Oils Although ghee (clarified butter) is the fat traditionally used in Indian cooking, the recipes in this book use healthier sunflower and vegetable oils. These oils have a mild flavour, so do not interfere with the subtle spicing and other flavourings of the dishes.

Pulses A good stock of dried and tinned pulses are essential for the storecupboard. Dried lentils, split peas and pale green mung beans need no soaking and do not take long to cook, while beans such as chickpeas, black-eyed beans and kidney beans require lengthy soaking and boiling until tender. For these 'high-maintenance' pulses, it is worth buying the organic, tinned variety to save time. Buy them tinned in water, rather than brine, and rinse them well before adding to the pan.

Rice The best rice to serve with curry is basmati. It has a fragrant aroma and light fluffy texture. It benefits from rinsing or soaking in cold water before cooking. Thai jasmine rice should be served with the green and red Thai curries.

chicken

All too often, we rely on chicken for the basis of an evening meal without really knowing how to make the best of this healthy, satisfying meat. The good news is it's perfect in a curry – and it's so versatile an ingredient that there are lots of flavours and textures that marry well with it. Imagine tender pieces of chicken thigh and succulent tiger prawns simmering in curried coconut milk, then spooned onto rice noodles and topped with all sorts of condiments, and you have the fabulous **Mandalay chicken noodle curry (page 15)** – a dish my good friends in Mumbai often serve up for Sunday lunch because there is so much to savour within one bowl. Meanwhile, it's well known that **chicken tikka masala (page 12)** is top of Britain's list of favourite dishes, while **Thai green chicken curry (page 17)** is increasingly being served up in homes around the country for its delicate aromatics and fresh ingredients. The lesser known **Vietnamese chicken curry (page 21)** illustrates that curries needn't mean chunks of meat swimming in gravy but rather the transformation of a handful of spices into a concentrated sauce, verging on alchemy. For fuss-free suppers, **chicken & spinach curry (page 14)** and **butter chicken (page 18)** are left to marinate overnight, so that most of the work is done by the time you get round to cooking the next day.

chicken tikka masala

Boneless, marinated chicken pieces are grilled, then added to a rich, creamy, tomato-based sauce. Serve with warm Naan (page 85) or steamed basmati rice.

4 boneless, skinless chicken breasts, cut into bite-sized pieces

salt and freshly ground black pepper

freshly chopped coriander leaves, to garnish

sliced red chillies, to garnish (optional)

chicken tikka marinade

250 g natural yoghurt

1 tablespoon freshly squeezed lemon juice

2 teaspoons ground cumin

1 teaspoon ground cinnamon

2 teaspoons cayenne pepper

2 teaspoons freshly ground black pepper

1 tablespoon finely grated fresh ginger

tikka masala sauce

1 tablespoon butter

1 garlic clove, crushed

1 red chilli (deseeded if desired), finely chopped

2 teaspoons ground cumin

3 teaspoons paprika

200 g tinned chopped tomatoes

2 tablespoons tomato purée

200 ml double cream

serves 4

To make the chicken tikka marinade, combine the yoghurt, lemon juice, cumin, cinnamon, cayenne, black pepper and ginger in a large glass bowl and season with salt. Stir in the chicken, cover and refrigerate for 4–6 hours or overnight.

Thread the marinated chicken on to metal skewers (discarding the marinade). Cook under a hot, preheated grill for about 5 minutes on each side.

Meanwhile, make the tikka masala sauce. Melt the butter in a large, heavy frying pan over medium heat. Sauté the garlic and chilli for 1 minute. Add the cumin and paprika and season well.

Purée the tinned tomatoes in a blender until smooth, then add to the pan with the cream. Simmer over low heat until sauce has thickened, about 20 minutes.

Add the grilled chicken to the pan and simmer for 10 minutes, or until cooked through. Transfer to a serving platter and garnish with the coriander and chillies, if using. Serve with warm naan or steamed basmati rice.

chicken & spinach curry

Serve this velvety chicken and spinach curry with steamed basmati rice and Onion, Cucumber & Tomato Relish (page 88).

To make the marinade, combine the yoghurt, garlic, ginger, coriander and curry powder in a large glass bowl and season well. Stir in the chicken, cover and refrigerate for 3–4 hours or overnight.

Put the spinach in a saucepan and cook for 8–10 minutes. Drain thoroughly, place in a food processor and blend until smooth. Season well.

Heat the sunflower oil in a large, non-stick frying pan and add the onion. Cook over gentle heat for 10–12 minutes. Add the cumin seeds and stir-fry for 1–2 minutes.

Increase the heat to high and add the marinated chicken (discarding the marinade). Stir-fry for 6–8 minutes. Pour in the stock and spinach and bring to the boil. Reduce the heat to low, cover tightly and cook for 25–30 minutes, or until the chicken is cooked through.

Uncover the pan, check the seasoning and cook over high heat for 3–4 minutes, stirring often. Remove from the heat and stir in the lemon juice. Serve immediately with steamed basmati rice and Onion, Cucumber & Tomato Relish.

800 g boneless, skinless chicken thighs, cut into bite-sized pieces

500 g frozen spinach, thawed

2 tablespoons sunflower oil

1 onion, finely chopped

2 teaspoons cumin seeds

150 ml chicken stock

1 tablespoon freshly squeezed lemon juice

salt and freshly ground black pepper

marinade

100 g natural yoghurt

2 tablespoons crushed garlic

2 tablespoons finely grated fresh ginger

2 tablespoons ground coriander

2 tablespoons medium curry powder

serves 4

Mandalay chicken noodle curry

Also known as 'khow sway', this delicious Burmese curry is the perfect choice for relaxed entertaining. If you can't find Burmese shrimp paste in the supermarket, use 1 tablespoon dark soy sauce instead.

800 g boneless, skinless chicken thighs, cut into bite-sized pieces

2 large onions, roughly chopped

5 garlic cloves, roughly chopped

1 teaspoon finely grated fresh ginger

2 tablespoons sunflower oil

½ teaspoon Burmese shrimp paste (belacan)

400 ml tinned coconut milk

2 tablespoons medium curry powder

200 g uncooked tiger prawns, shelled and deveined

200 g rice vermicelli

salt and freshly ground black pepper

to garnish

freshly chopped coriander leaves

finely chopped red onion

fried garlic slivers

sliced red chillies

lime wedges

serves 4

Season the chicken and set aside.

Put the onions, garlic and ginger in a food processor and blend until smooth (you might need to add a couple of tablespoons of water).

Heat the sunflower oil in a large saucepan. Add the onion mixture and shrimp paste and cook over high heat, stirring, for about 5 minutes.

Add the chicken and cook over medium heat, stirring, until it browns. Add the coconut milk and curry powder and bring to the boil. Reduce the heat, cover and simmer for about 40 minutes. Stir occasionally.

Stir in the prawns and cook, uncovered, for 6–8 minutes, or until pink and cooked through.

Put the noodles in a bowl, cover with boiling water and leave for 10 minutes. Drain and divide between 4 large, warmed bowls. Ladle the curry over the top and garnish with the coriander, red onion, garlic, chillies and lime wedges.

Thai green chicken curry

Pea aubergines are available from good oriental supermarkets. If you can't get hold of them, substitute with regular aubergines, cut into bite-sized pieces. Serve with steamed Thai jasmine rice.

Heat the sunflower oil in a large non-stick wok or saucepan and add the curry paste and chillies. Stir-fry for 2–3 minutes, then add the chicken. Stir and cook for 5–6 minutes, or until the chicken is sealed and lightly browned.

Stir in the coconut milk, stock, lime leaves, fish sauce, palm sugar and pea aubergines. Simmer, uncovered, for 10–15 minutes, stirring occasionally.

Add the green beans and bamboo shoots and continue to simmer for 6–8 minutes.

Remove from the heat and stir in the basil, coriander and lime juice. Serve with steamed Thai jasmine rice.

1 tablespoon sunflower oil

3 tablespoons Thai green curry paste

2 green chillies, finely chopped

800 g boneless, skinless chicken thighs, cut into bite-sized pieces

400 ml tinned coconut milk

200 ml chicken stock

6 kaffir lime leaves

2 tablespoons fish sauce

1 tablespoon grated palm sugar

200 g pea aubergines

100 g green beans, halved

50 g tinned sliced bamboo shoots, drained and rinsed

a large handful of fresh Thai sweet basil leaves

a large handful of fresh coriander leaves

freshly squeezed juice of 1 lime

serves 4

butter chicken

This popular chicken curry, natively called 'makhani' has its origins in the Mughal dynasty. It is rich and very moreish. Serve with steamed basmati rice or warm Naan (page 85).

To make the marinade, heat a non-stick frying pan and toast the cashew nuts, fennel seeds, cinnamon, coriander, cardamom seeds, peppercorns and cloves for 2–3 minutes, or until very aromatic. Transfer to a spice grinder and grind until smooth.

Add this mixture to a blender with the garlic, ginger, vinegar, tomato purée and half the yoghurt and process until smooth. Transfer to a large glass bowl with the remaining yoghurt. Stir in the chicken, cover and refrigerate for 24 hours.

Melt the butter in a large, non-stick wok or saucepan and add the onion, cassia bark and cardamom pods. Stir-fry over medium heat for 6–8 minutes, or until the onion has softened. Add the marinated chicken (discarding the marinade) and cook, stirring, for 10 minutes. Season.

Stir in the chilli powder, tinned tomatoes and stock, bring to the boil, then reduce the heat to low. Simmer, uncovered, for 40–45 minutes, stirring occasionally.

Add the cream and cook gently for a further 4–5 minutes. Garnish with the coriander and serve immediately with steamed basmati rice or naan.

800 g boneless, skinless chicken thighs, cut into large bite-sized pieces

50 g butter

1 large onion, finely chopped

1 cassia bark or cinnamon stick

4 cardamom pods

1 teaspoon mild or medium chilli powder

400 g tinned chopped tomatoes

150 ml chicken stock

100 ml single cream

salt and freshly ground black pepper

freshly chopped coriander, to garnish

marinade

150 g cashew nuts

1 tablespoon fennel seeds

2 teaspoons ground cinnamon

1 tablespoon ground coriander

1 teaspoon cardamom seeds, crushed

1 teaspoon black peppercorns

½ teaspoon ground cloves

4 garlic cloves, crushed

2 teaspoons finely grated fresh ginger

2 tablespoons white wine vinegar

100 g tomato purée

150 g natural yoghurt

serves 4

Vietnamese chicken curry

Even though Vietnam was colonized by the French, the traditional cuisine has more in common with their Chinese neighbours. Ground bean sauce is available in good Asian supermarkets but if you can't find it, substitute oyster sauce instead.

3 tablespoons sunflower oil

800 g skinless chicken breasts, cut into thin strips

12 spring onions, cut into 3-cm lengths

4 garlic cloves, finely chopped

1 red chilli, thinly sliced

2 star anise

4 tablespoons very finely chopped lemongrass

1 teaspoon cardamom seeds, crushed

1 cinnamon stick

300 g green beans, halved

1 carrot, cut into batons

2 tablespoons fish sauce

2 tablespoons ground bean sauce

a small handful of fresh coriander leaves, chopped

a small handful of fresh mint leaves, chopped

chopped roasted peanuts, to serve

serves 4

Heat half the sunflower oil in a large, non-stick frying pan and stir-fry the chicken, in batches, for 1–2 minutes. Remove with a slotted spoon and keep warm.

Heat the remaining oil in the same frying pan and stir-fry the spring onions for 1–2 minutes, or until softened. Add the garlic, chilli, star anise, lemongrass, cardamom seeds, cinnamon, green beans and carrots. Stir-fry for 6–8 minutes.

Return the chicken to the pan with the fish sauce and ground bean sauce. Stir-fry for 3–4 minutes, or until the chicken is cooked through. Remove from the heat and sprinkle over the coriander, mint and peanuts before serving.

meat

For gutsy stews which take their time on the hob to produce deep flavours and melt-in-the-mouth lamb, beef or pork, meat curries are second to none. Every region of India excels in its own version which has been shaped by many different influences. **Vindaloo (page 34)** hails from Goa, once colonized by the Portuguese who brought with them a pork stew from which the Indian vindaloo was born. This, along with others like **beef madras (page 33)**, is often erroneously touted as fierce and fiery, but you can adjust the heat to suit your tastes – from deseeding the chillies to lessen their heat, to using mild chilli powder. It's good to know that curries are flexible in this way, and it is often the case that the meats used are interchangeable too. So the **kofta curry (page 27)** and even the **lamb korma (page 29)** offer a choice of meat. A word of advice: many meat curries, particularly the **lamb rogan josh (page 24)** taste even better the day after they are made, so if you can resist the temptation to eat the whole lot in one sitting, you will really notice when the spices have melded and mellowed the next day. If you're entertaining, there's a meat dish for every occasion. **Kashmiri lamb kebabs (page 28)** are ideal for a barbecue, while the **mince & pea curry (page 30)** is left to simmer for over an hour leaving you free to enjoy your guests' company.

lamb rogan josh

This slow-cooked lamb stew from Kashmir in north India is perfect for hassle-free entertaining as it almost cooks itself!

Heat half the sunflower oil in a large, heavy-based casserole dish and cook the lamb, in batches, for 3–4 minutes, until evenly browned. Remove with a slotted spoon and set aside.

Add the remaining oil to the dish and add the onions. Cook over medium heat for 10–12 minutes, stirring often, until soft and lightly browned.

Add the garlic, ginger, cassia, chilli powder, paprika and cardamom pods. Stir-fry for 1–2 minutes, then add the curry paste and lamb. Stir-fry for 2–3 minutes, then stir in the tinned tomatoes, tomato purée, sugar, stock and potatoes. Season well and bring to the boil. Reduce the heat to very low (using a heat diffuser if possible) and cover tightly. Simmer gently for 2–2½ hours, or until the lamb is meltingly tender.

Remove from the heat and garnish with the coriander and a drizzle of yoghurt.

2 tablespoons sunflower oil

800 g boneless lamb shoulder, cut into large bite-sized pieces

2 large onions, thickly sliced

3 garlic cloves, crushed

2 teaspoons finely grated fresh ginger

2 cassia barks or cinnamon sticks

2 teaspoons Kashmiri chilli powder

2 teaspoons paprika

6 cardamom pods

4 tablespoons medium curry paste

400 g tinned chopped tomatoes

6 tablespoons tomato purée

1 teaspoon sugar

400 ml lamb stock

4–6 potatoes, peeled and left whole

freshly chopped coriander leaves, to garnish

whisked natural yoghurt, to drizzle

serves 4

kofta curry

Every country seems to have their own version of the 'kofta' or meatball. Here the meatballs are cooked in a spicy tomato sauce that is perfect served with warm Naan (page 85) or steamed basmati rice.

To make the koftas, put the ginger, garlic, cinnamon, coriander and mince in a mixing bowl. Season well and, using your fingers, mix well to combine. Roll tablespoons of the mixture into bite-sized balls, place on a tray, cover and chill for 1–2 hours.

Heat 2 tablespoons of the sunflower oil in a large, non-stick frying pan, then add the koftas and cook in batches until lightly browned. Remove with a slotted spoon and set aside.

Add the remaining oil to the pan and place over medium heat. Add the onion and stir-fry for 4–5 minutes, then stir in the curry paste. Stir-fry for 1–2 minutes, then add the tinned tomatoes and stock. Bring to the boil, reduce the heat to low and leave to simmer gently, uncovered, for 10–15 minutes.

Add the koftas to the pan and stir carefully to coat them in the sauce. Simmer gently for 10–15 minutes, or until cooked through. Stir in the cream and cook for a final 2–3 minutes. Remove from the heat and garnish with the extra coriander leaves. Serve with warm naan or steamed basmati rice.

3 tablespoons sunflower oil
1 onion, finely chopped
2 tablespoons medium curry paste
400 g tinned chopped tomatoes
200 ml chicken stock
150 ml double cream

koftas

2 teaspoons finely grated fresh ginger
4 teaspoons crushed garlic
1 teaspoon ground cinnamon
8 tablespoons freshly chopped coriander leaves, plus extra to garnish
800 g minced lamb, beef or pork

serves 4

Kashmiri lamb kebabs

These succulent kebabs make for effortless entertaining, as they can be marinated up to 48 hours in advance and take a short time to cook. You can substitute the lamb with boneless beef, pork or chicken. Serve with Onion, Cucumber & Tomato Relish and Coriander & Mint Chutney (both page 88).

800 g lamb neck fillet, cut into bite-sized pieces
salt and freshly ground black pepper

marinade
2 shallots, finely chopped
2 teaspoons crushed garlic
2 teaspoons finely grated fresh ginger
1 tablespoon ground cumin
1 tablespoon ground coriander
1 tablespoon Kashmiri chilli powder
1 tablespoon fennel seeds
6 tablespoons freshly chopped coriander leaves
2 tablespoons freshly chopped mint leaves
250 ml double cream
½ teaspoon sugar

8–12 metal skewers
a baking tray, lined with non-stick baking parchment

serves 4

Put the lamb in a large glass bowl. Put all the marinade ingredients in a food processor and blend until smooth. Season well. Pour over the lamb, cover and marinate in the fridge for 24–48 hours.

When ready to cook, remove the bowl from the fridge and leave to come to room temperature.

Preheat the oven to 200°C (400°F) Gas 6.

When ready to cook, thread the marinated lamb on to 8–12 metal skewers and arrange on the prepared baking tray. Place in the preheated oven and cook for 12–15 minutes, or until tender and cooked through.

Serve with Onion, Cucumber & Tomato Relish and Coriander & Mint Chutney.

lamb korma

This mild and creamy dish works equally well if you substitute the lamb for chicken. Serve with warm Naan (page 85) or steamed basmati rice.

4 tablespoons vegetable oil

800 g lamb neck fillet, thinly sliced

1 onion, finely chopped

2 garlic cloves, finely chopped

2 teaspoons finely grated fresh ginger

80 g ground almonds

1 tablespoon white poppy seeds (optional)

5 tablespoons Korma curry paste

150 ml lamb or chicken stock

250 ml single cream

2 tablespoons finely chopped pistachio nuts

1 tablespoon golden sultanas

salt and freshly ground black pepper

crispy fried onions, to garnish

serves 4

Heat half the vegetable oil in a large, non-stick frying pan and brown the lamb, in batches, for 2–3 minutes. Remove with a slotted spoon and set aside. Add the remaining oil to the pan and cook the onion, garlic and ginger over medium heat for 3–4 minutes.

Stir in the almonds, poppy seeds, if using, and curry paste and stir-fry for 1–2 minutes.

Add the lamb to the pan with the stock and cream. Bring to the boil. Reduce the heat to low, season well and simmer, uncovered, for 30–40 minutes, stirring occasionally, until the lamb is tender.

Remove from the heat, stir in the pistachio nuts and sultanas and garnish with crispy fried onions. Serve with warm naan or steamed basmati rice.

mince & pea curry

Minced meat is cooked slowly with spices and peas resulting in a subtle, fragrant curry called 'kheema mutter', which is great when accompanied by Tarka Dal (page 69), steamed basmati rice or bread.

2 tablespoons sunflower oil

1 large onion, finely chopped

3 garlic cloves, crushed

1 teaspoon finely grated fresh ginger

3–4 green chillies (deseeded if desired), thinly sliced

1 tablespoon cumin seeds

3 tablespoons medium curry paste

800 g minced beef

400 g tinned chopped tomatoes

1 teaspoon sugar

4 tablespoons tomato purée

4 tablespoons coconut cream

250 g frozen or fresh peas

salt and freshly ground black pepper

a large handful of fresh coriander leaves, chopped, to garnish

serves 4

Heat the sunflower oil in a large, heavy-based saucepan and add the onion. Cook over low heat for 15–20 minutes, until softened and just turning light golden. Add the garlic, ginger, chillies, cumin seeds and curry paste and stir-fry over high heat for 1–2 minutes.

Add the minced beef and stir-fry for 3–4 minutes, then stir in the tinned tomatoes, sugar, and tomato purée and bring to the boil. Season well, cover and reduce the heat to low. Cook for 1–1½ hours. 10 minutes before the end of the cooking time, add the coconut cream and peas.

To serve, garnish with the coriander and serve with Tarka Dal, steamed basmati rice or bread.

beef madras

This fiery curry from southern India is not for the faint-hearted although you can decrease the amounts of chilli and curry powder to suit your palate. Serve with pickles as well as steamed basmati rice, if you like.

To make the marinade, combine the yoghurt and curry powder in a glass bowl. Stir in the beef, season with salt, cover and marinate in the fridge for 24 hours.

Heat the sunflower oil in a large, non-stick wok or frying pan and add the bay leaf, cinnamon, cloves and cardamom pods. Stir-fry for 1 minute, then add the onion. Stir-fry over medium heat for 4–5 minutes, then add the garlic, ginger, turmeric, red chilli, chilli powder and cumin. Add the marinated beef (discarding the marinade) and stir-fry for 10–15 minutes over low heat.

Pour in the tinned tomatoes and coconut milk and bring to the boil. Reduce the heat to low, cover tightly and simmer gently for 1 hour, stirring occasionally. Stir in the garam masala 5 minutes before the end of cooking.

Check the seasoning. Drizzle with extra coconut milk and garnish with the coriander. Serve immediately with steamed basmati rice.

800 g stewing beef, cut into large bite-sized pieces

2 tablespoons sunflower oil

1 dried bay leaf

1 cinnamon stick

3 cloves

4 cardamom pods, bruised

1 large onion, thinly sliced

3 garlic cloves, crushed

1 teaspoon finely grated fresh ginger

1 teaspoon ground turmeric

1 red chilli, split in half lengthways

2 teaspoons hot chilli powder

2 teaspoons ground cumin

200 g tinned chopped tomatoes

300 ml coconut milk, plus extra to drizzle

¼ teaspoon garam masala

salt and freshly ground black pepper

a small handful of fresh coriander leaves, chopped, to garnish

marinade

5 tablespoons natural yoghurt

3 tablespoons Madras curry powder

serves 4

pork vindaloo

This fiery curry originates from the former Portuguese colony of Goa. The name is derived from the Portuguese for vinegar and garlic, the curry's main ingredients. Serve with steamed basmati rice.

To make the spice paste, put all the ingredients in a small food processor and blend to a paste. Transfer to a large glass bowl and add the pork. Rub the paste all over the pork pieces, cover and marinate in the fridge for up to 24 hours.

To make the vindaloo, heat the sunflower oil in a large, heavy-based saucepan, then add the onion. Stir-fry for 3–4 minutes, then add the chilli powder, turmeric, cumin and marinated pork (discarding the spice paste). Stir-fry for 3–4 minutes, then stir in the potatoes, tomato purée, sugar, tinned tomatoes and stock. Season well and bring to the boil. Cover tightly and reduce the heat to low. Simmer gently for 1½ hours.

800 g boneless pork shoulder, cut into bite-sized pieces

salt and freshly ground black pepper

spice paste

2 teaspoons cumin seeds, toasted in a dry frying pan

6 dried red chillies, broken into pieces

1 teaspoon cardamom seeds, crushed

1 cassia bark or cinnamon stick

10 black peppercorns

8 garlic cloves, finely grated

5 tablespoons white wine vinegar

vindaloo

2 tablespoons sunflower oil

1 onion, finely chopped

1 tablespoon medium or hot chilli powder

1 teaspoon ground turmeric

2 teaspoons ground cumin

4 large potatoes, peeled and cut into chunks

6 tablespoons tomato purée

1 tablespoon sugar

400 g tinned chopped tomatoes

200 ml vegetable or chicken stock

serves 4

fish

Fish curries are particularly close to my heart. When I was a boy growing up in Mumbai, we had a cook responsible for making all the family meals, and Sunday was the only day my father was allowed (and time permitted him) to get in the kitchen and slave lovingly over a hot stove. So on that day we visited the food markets. Favourite among these was the fish market, from which we brought home just-caught fish and live crabs – these scraped and crawled on our kitchen table until it was time for them to jump into the cooking pot. As such, crab and fish curries such as **fish mollee (page 46)** have become cherished memories from my childhood. The sunny colour and zingy flavour of **Goan prawn curry (page 45)** are so incomparable that I seek it out before anything else whenever I go back to Goa. From delicate **tamarind & halibut curry (page 42)** to feisty **tandoori monkfish kebabs (page 38)** with its distinctively vibrant colouring, fish is infinitely versatile. And one of the greatest benefits of fish curries is their short cooking time: **lemongrass & scallop curry (page 43)** and the stunning **banana-leaf fish (page 41)** are guaranteed to become your favourite fast food. If you want all the punch of a curry but lighter, quicker and fresher, fish is the ideal choice: just like a taste of sunshine even on the rainiest of evenings.

tandoori monkfish kebabs

Succulent pieces of monkfish are marinated in a blend of spices and yoghurt, then quickly grilled. You could also barbecue these kebabs for an authentic smoky, tandoori flavour.

600 g monkfish tail fillets, cut into bite-sized pieces

4 red peppers, deseeded and cut into bite-sized pieces

freshly chopped coriander, to garnish

freshly chopped mint, to garnish

lime wedges, to serve

thinly sliced red onions, to serve

tandoori marinade

350 g natural yoghurt

2 tablespoons finely grated onion

1 tablespoon finely grated garlic

1 tablespoon finely grated fresh ginger

freshly squeezed juice of 2 limes

3 tablespoons tandoori spice powder or paste

4 tablespoons tomato purée

8 metal skewers

serves 4

To make the tandoori marinade, combine the yoghurt, onion, garlic, ginger, lime juice, tandoori spice powder or paste and tomato purée in a large glass bowl. Stir in the monkfish and red peppers, cover and refrigerate for 2–4 hours.

When ready to cook, thread the marinated monkfish and red peppers on to the skewers and cook under a preheated medium grill for 4–5 minutes on each side, or until the fish is just cooked through.

Garnish with the coriander and mint and serve with lime wedges and sliced red onions on the side.

banana-leaf fish

Known as 'patra ni macchi', these aromatic, banana-leaf wrapped fish parcels are a famous Parsi preparation. If you cannot get hold of banana leaves, use squares of oiled aluminium foil or baking parchment instead.

Preheat the oven to 200°C (400°F) Gas 6.

Cut the banana leaves into four 24-cm squares and soften them by dipping them in a pan of very hot water. Wipe the pieces dry when they are pliant.

To make the spice paste, grind the cumin, ground coriander, sugar, coconut, chillies, coriander, mint, garlic and ginger to a paste in a food processor or with a pestle and mortar.

Heat 1 tablespoon of the sunflower oil in a frying pan and cook the paste over low heat until aromatic. Season with salt.

Lay the banana-leaf squares on a work surface. Spread the paste liberally over both sides of each piece of fish. Drizzle the lime juice over the top. Place a piece of fish on each banana leaf and wrap up like a parcel, securing it with skewers or string. Place these parcels on a non-stick baking tray and bake in the preheated oven for 15–20 minutes, or until the fish is just cooked through. Open out each fish parcel on its plate.

fresh banana leaves

3 tablespoons sunflower oil

4 thick halibut fillets (about 200 g each), skinned

freshly squeezed juice of 2 limes

salt

spice paste

2 teaspoons ground cumin

2 teaspoons ground coriander

1½ teaspoons golden caster sugar

150 g freshly grated coconut

4 green chillies, deseeded and chopped

8–10 tablespoons freshly chopped coriander leaves

4 tablespoons freshly chopped mint leaves

5 garlic cloves, chopped

1 teaspoon finely grated fresh ginger

metal skewers or kitchen string

serves 4

tamarind & halibut curry

This hearty curry can also be made with any thick, firm fish fillets, such as cod or salmon. Serve with steamed basmati rice and poppadoms, if you like.

To make the marinade, combine the tamarind paste, vinegar, cumin seeds, turmeric, chilli powder and salt in a shallow glass bowl. Stir in the fish, cover and refrigerate for 25–30 minutes.

Meanwhile, heat a wok or large frying pan over high heat and add the sunflower oil. Add the onion, garlic, ginger and mustard seeds, reduce the heat to low and cook for 10 minutes, stirring occasionally.

Add the tinned tomatoes and sugar and bring to the boil. Reduce the heat, cover and cook gently for 15–20 minutes, stirring occasionally.

Add the fish and its marinade and stir gently to mix. Cover and simmer gently for 15–20 minutes, or until the fish is cooked through and flakes easily. Serve with steamed basmati rice and poppadoms.

750 g thick halibut fillets, skinned and cubed

4 tablespoons sunflower oil

1 onion, finely chopped

3 garlic cloves, crushed

2 tablespoons finely grated fresh ginger

2 teaspoons black mustard seeds

two 400-g tins chopped tomatoes

1 teaspoon sugar

marinade

1 tablespoon tamarind paste

60 ml rice wine vinegar

2 tablespoons cumin seeds

1 teaspoon ground turmeric

1 teaspoon mild or medium chilli powder

1 teaspoon salt

serves 4

lemongrass & scallop curry

Very fragrant and aromatic, this delicious curry is quick to whip up. Make sure you use only the freshest scallops.

Put the chilli powder, ground coriander, cumin, garlic, shallots, lemongrass, galangal, palm sugar, shrimp paste, peanuts and coconut milk in a blender and process until fairly smooth.

Put a large wok or frying pan over high heat and add the spice mixture. Bring to the boil, reduce the heat to low and simmer gently, uncovered, for 12–15 minutes, stirring occasionally.

Add the scallops and bring back to the boil. Reduce the heat to low and simmer gently for 6–8 minutes or until the scallops are cooked through. Remove from the heat and scatter over some Thai basil leaves, chopped roasted peanuts and chopped red chillies before serving.

1 tablespoon mild or medium chilli powder

1 teaspoon ground coriander

2 teaspoons ground cumin

2 garlic cloves, crushed

6 small shallots, finely chopped

6 tablespoons finely chopped lemongrass

1 teaspoon finely grated galangal

1 tablespoon grated palm sugar

½ teaspoon shrimp paste

2 tablespoons finely chopped unroasted peanuts

600 ml coconut milk

1 kg raw scallops, cleaned

Thai sweet basil leaves, to garnish

chopped roasted peanuts, to garnish

chopped, deseeded red chillies, to garnish

serves 4

2 tablespoons sunflower oil

2 onions, finely chopped

1 tablespoon finely grated fresh ginger

4 garlic cloves, crushed

2 red chillies (deseeded if desired), thinly sliced

¼ teaspoon ground turmeric

2 teaspoons ground coriander

1 teaspoon medium or hot chilli powder

2 teaspoons ground cumin

1 tablespoon tamarind paste

200 ml coconut milk

1 teaspoon jaggery or soft brown sugar

1 kg uncooked tiger prawns, shelled and deveined but tails left intact

freshly chopped coriander, to garnish

lime wedges, to serve

serves 4

Heat the sunflower oil in a large saucepan and add the onions. Cook over medium heat for 4–5 minutes, or until softened. Add the ginger, garlic and chillies and stir-fry for 1–2 minutes.

Add the turmeric, ground coriander, chilli powder and cumin and stir-fry for 1–2 minutes.

Add the tamarind paste and coconut milk along with 300 ml water and bring to the boil. Add the jaggery, reduce the heat to low and simmer gently for 15–20 minutes.

Add the prawns to the pan and cook over high heat for 4–5 minutes, or until they turn pink and are cooked through. Season and remove from the heat. Garnish with the coriander. Serve with lime wedges, steamed basmati rice and poppadoms.

Goan prawn curry

This simple and delicious prawn curry evokes pictures of warm seas, sandy beaches and swaying palm trees. Serve with steamed basmati rice and poppadoms and wash it all down with an ice-cold beer for maximum indulgence.

fish mollee

Kerala on the west coast of India is home to this creamy, mild and very flavoursome fish curry. Use any firm, thick white fish or prawns as you like. Serve with steamed basmati rice.

Put the onion, garlic, chillies, cumin, ground coriander, turmeric, fresh coriander and 200 ml water in a food processor and blend until smooth.

Heat the sunflower oil in a large, heavy-based frying pan, add the curry leaves and stir-fry for 20–30 seconds. Add the blended mixture, stir and cook over high heat for 3–4 minutes. Turn the heat to low, add the coconut milk and simmer gently, uncovered, for 20 minutes.

Add the fish to the pan in a single layer and bring the mixture back to the boil. Reduce the heat to low and simmer gently for 5–6 minutes, or until the fish is just cooked through. Season and remove from the heat. Garnish with deep-fried curry leaves and serve with steamed basmati rice.

1 onion, coarsely chopped

4 garlic cloves, crushed

2 green chillies, deseeded and finely chopped

1 tablespoon ground cumin

1 teaspoon ground coriander

1 teaspoon ground turmeric

30 g fresh coriander leaves, finely chopped

2 tablespoons sunflower oil

6 fresh curry leaves

400 ml coconut milk

salt and freshly ground black pepper

4 thick halibut or cod fillets (about 200 g each), skinned

deep-fried curry leaves, to garnish

serves 4

vegetables

From Kerala in the southern tip of India, via Mumbai on the western coast, to Punjab in the north and a leap eastwards to Thailand, Asia has a treasure trove of vegetable curries on offer: try deep, heady, tomatoey **spiced aubergines (page 51)** or the delicate fragrance of **vegetable stew (page 56)** – both guarantee an explosion of flavours in your mouth. And take inspiration from street vendors all over India who sell snacks such as **onion bhajis (page 61)** and **spicy potato balls (page 60)** stuffed in a roll with chutney. Side dish **(saag paneer, page 62)** or vegetarian option **(okra masala, page 55)**, there is a vegetable recipe to suit every mood and occasion. If you want to do as Indians do, you must include a vegetable dish, such as **cauliflower masala (page 52)** with your curry. In India, a typical meal consists of rice, bread, vegetables, dal and a meat or fish curry, all served at the same time, and all there to provide a spectrum of taste sensations. So next time you are planning a feast for friends, why not surprise everyone with a flaming **Thai red pumpkin curry (page 59)** or a simple **tomato & egg curry (page 53)** and a host of accompaniments – swap roast potatoes for **spiced potatoes (page 62)** and boring boiled cabbage for beautifully spiced **Punjabi cabbage (page 65)**. You'll find every plate scraped clean at the end of the meal!

spiced aubergines

Aubergines are cooked in pickling spices in this warming dish. Serve it with yoghurt and steamed basmati rice and it becomes an ideal vegetarian main course.

Put the ginger, garlic and half the tinned tomatoes in a blender and blend until smooth. Set aside.

Heat half the sunflower oil in a large, heavy-based frying pan, then add as many aubergines as you can fit in a single layer, cut-side down. Cook over medium heat for 3–4 minutes, or until lightly browned, then turn over and cook for a further 3–4 minutes. Remove with a slotted spoon and drain on kitchen paper. Repeat with the remaining oil and cook the remaining aubergines. Remove from the pan and drain on kitchen paper.

Reheat the oil that is left in the frying pan and add the fennel seeds and nigella seeds. Stir-fry for 1–2 minutes, then add the blended tomato mixture. Stir-fry for 2–3 minutes, then add the remaining tinned tomatoes, the coriander, turmeric and paprika. Season well. Cook over medium heat, stirring often, for 6–8 minutes, until the mixture is smooth and thick.

Add the reserved aubergines to the pan and toss gently until evenly coated. Cover and cook gently for 10–12 minutes. Remove from the heat and leave to rest for 10–15 minutes before serving. Garnish with the coriander and serve with steamed basmati rice and a little yoghurt on the side.

1 tablespoon finely grated fresh ginger

2 tablespoons crushed garlic

400 g tinned chopped tomatoes

250 ml sunflower oil

750 g baby aubergines, halved lengthways

2 teaspoons fennel seeds

2 teaspoons nigella seeds

1 tablespoon ground coriander

¼ teaspoon ground turmeric

1 teaspoon paprika

salt and freshly ground black pepper

freshly chopped coriander leaves, to garnish

serves 4

cauliflower masala

In this simple dish, cauliflower florets are stir-fried in a seasoned, spiced oil until just tender. Substitute broccoli florets if desired, to ring the changes.

1 tablespoon sunflower oil

2 teaspoons cumin seeds

1 teaspoon black mustard seeds

500 g cauliflower florets

2 garlic cloves, thinly sliced

2 teaspoons finely chopped
fresh ginger

1 green chilli, thinly sliced

1 teaspoon garam masala

150 ml hot water

freshly squeezed juice of ½ lemon

salt and freshly ground black pepper

serves 4

Heat the sunflower oil in a large frying pan over medium heat. Add the cumin seeds and mustard seeds. Stir-fry for 30 seconds, then add the cauliflower, garlic, ginger and chilli. Turn the heat to high and stir-fry for 6–8 minutes, or until the cauliflower is lightly browned at the edges.

Stir in the garam masala and hot water and stir well. Cover and cook over high heat for 1–2 minutes.

Season well and drizzle with the lemon juice just before serving.

tomato & egg curry

This tasty curry from Mumbai is quick to prepare and makes good use of everyday kitchen staples. Serve with steamed basmati rice.

4 potatoes, peeled and cut into bite-sized pieces

2 tablespoons sunflower oil

1 tablespoon black mustard seeds

2 garlic cloves, crushed

2 dried red chillies

10 fresh curry leaves

1 onion, thinly sliced

2 tablespoons medium curry powder

1 tablespoon ground coriander

1 tablespoon cumin seeds

½ teaspoon ground turmeric

400 g tinned chopped tomatoes

1 teaspoon sugar

200 ml coconut milk

8 eggs, hardboiled and peeled

salt

serves 4

Cook the potatoes in a pan of salted boiling water until tender.

Heat the sunflower oil in a large, non-stick wok or frying pan. Add the mustard seeds and when they start to pop, add the garlic, chillies and curry leaves and sauté for 1 minute. Add the onion and cook, stirring constantly, for 5–6 minutes.

Stir in the curry powder, coriander, cumin seeds and turmeric, then stir in the tinned tomatoes and sugar. Bring to the boil, reduce the heat to medium and cook for 8–10 minutes, stirring often.

Add the coconut milk, eggs and potatoes. Cook gently for 8–10 minutes, until the sauce has thickened. Season with salt and serve with steamed basmati rice.

okra masala

When shopping for the okra, make sure that they are bright green, firm and not bruised. This dish makes a fantastic vegetarian main course when accompanied by steamed basmati rice, dal and pickles.

Heat the sunflower oil in a large, non-stick wok or frying pan over medium heat and add the curry leaves, mustard seeds and onion. Stir-fry for 3–4 minutes, then add the cumin, coriander, curry powder and turmeric. Stir-fry for 1–2 minutes, then add the garlic and okra. Stir and cook over high heat for 2–3 minutes.

Stir in the tomatoes and season well. Cover, reduce the heat to low and cook gently for 10–12 minutes, stirring occasionally, until the okra is tender.

Garnish with the grated coconut before serving with steamed basmati rice, dal and pickles.

2 tablespoons sunflower oil

6–8 fresh curry leaves

2 teaspoons black mustard seeds

1 onion, finely diced

2 teaspoons ground cumin

1 teaspoon ground coriander

2 teaspoons medium curry powder

1 teaspoon ground turmeric

3 garlic cloves, finely chopped

500 g okra, trimmed and cut diagonally into 2.5-cm pieces

2 ripe plum tomatoes, finely chopped

3 tablespoons freshly grated coconut

serves 4

vegetable stew

This fragrant and mild vegetable and coconut stew is called 'avial' in its home town of Kerala, in the southern tip of India. Traditionally served with steamed rice pancakes, it is equally good eaten with rice or bread.

2 tablespoons sunflower oil

6 shallots, thinly sliced

2 teaspoons black mustard seeds

8–10 fresh curry leaves

1 green chilli, thinly sliced

2 teaspoons finely grated fresh ginger

1 teaspoon ground turmeric

2 teaspoons ground cumin

6 black peppercorns

2 carrots, cut into thick batons

1 courgette, cut into thick batons

200 g green beans

1 large potato, peeled and cut into thick batons

300 ml coconut milk

100 ml vegetable stock or water

freshly squeezed juice of ½ lemon

salt and freshly ground black pepper

serves 4

Heat the sunflower oil in a large, heavy-based frying pan and add the shallots. Stir and cook over medium heat for 4–5 minutes. Add the mustard seeds, curry leaves, chilli, ginger, turmeric, cumin and peppercorns and stir-fry for 1–2 minutes.

Add the carrots, courgette, beans and potato to the pan along with the coconut milk and stock and bring to the boil. Reduce the heat, cover and cook gently for 12–15 minutes, or until the vegetables are tender.

Season well and drizzle with the lemon juice just before serving with steamed basmati rice or bread.

Thai red pumpkin curry

You can use butternut squash in this curry instead of the pumpkin if you prefer. To elaborate on the dish for a dinner party, throw in some cooked king prawns 5 minutes before the end of the cooking time.

Heat the sunflower oil in a large, non-stick wok or frying pan. Add the onion, garlic and ginger and stir-fry for 3–4 minutes. Stir in the curry paste and pumpkin and stir-fry for 3–4 minutes.

Pour in the coconut milk, stock, lime leaves, palm sugar and lemongrass. Bring to the boil, then reduce the heat to low and simmer gently for 20–25 minutes, stirring occasionally, or until the pumpkin is tender.

Season well and garnish with the Thai basil leaves and shredded lime leaves just before serving.

2 tablespoons sunflower oil

1 red onion, thinly sliced

2 garlic cloves, crushed

1 teaspoon finely grated fresh ginger

3 tablespoons Thai red curry paste

800 g pumpkin flesh, cut into bite-sized pieces

400 ml coconut milk

150 ml vegetable stock

6 kaffir lime leaves, plus extra, shredded, to garnish

2 teaspoons grated palm sugar

3 lemongrass stalks, bruised

salt and freshly ground black pepper

Thai sweet basil leaves, to garnish

serves 4

spicy potato balls

This savoury potato snack, called 'batata vadas', is a popular street food all over India. Serve them with a bowl of the Coriander & Mint Chutney (page 88) for dipping.

Cook the potatoes in a pan of salted boiling water until tender.

Heat the sunflower oil in a large frying pan over medium heat, then add the cumin seeds and mustard seeds and stir-fry for 1–2 minutes. Add the onion, ginger and chillies and stir-fry for 3–4 minutes. Add the potatoes and peas and stir-fry for 3–4 minutes. Season and stir in the lemon juice and coriander. Divide the mixture into 20 portions and shape each one into a ball. Chill until ready to use.

Combine the gram flour and self-raising flour in a bowl. Season and stir in the turmeric and coriander seeds. Gradually whisk in 350 ml water to make a fairly smooth and thick batter.

Fill a heavy-based saucepan one-third full with sunflower oil and heat to 180°C or until a piece of bread dropped in sizzles and browns within 10 seconds. Dip the potato balls in the batter, then carefully lower them into the hot oil in batches. Deep-fry for 1–2 minutes, or until golden. Drain on kitchen paper and serve warm with Coriander & Mint Chutney.

600 g potatoes, peeled and diced

1 tablespoon sunflower oil, plus extra for deep-frying

4 teaspoons cumin seeds

1 teaspoon black mustard seeds

1 small onion, finely chopped

2 teaspoons finely grated fresh ginger

2 green chillies, deseeded and chopped

200 g fresh peas

freshly squeezed juice of 1 lemon

6 tablespoons freshly chopped coriander leaves

100 g gram flour (besan)

80 g self-raising flour

a large pinch of ground turmeric

2 teaspoons coriander seeds, crushed

salt and freshly ground black pepper

makes 20

onion bhajis

A popular accompaniment to a takeaway curry, onion bhajis are irresistible. When they are freshly made and served with Cucumber & Yoghurt Relish (page 88), they make the perfect vegetarian snack food.

Combine the gram flour, chilli powder, turmeric, coriander seeds and a pinch of salt in a bowl. Gradually add enough water to make a thick batter which will hold the onion together. Mix the onions and curry leaves into the batter.

Fill a heavy-based saucepan one-third full with sunflower oil and heat to 180°C or until a piece of bread dropped in sizzles and browns within 10 seconds. Take spoonfuls of the onion batter and carefully lower them into the hot oil in batches. Deep-fry for 1–2 minutes, or until golden all over and cooked through. Drain on kitchen paper. Sprinkle with salt and serve warm with Cucumber & Yoghurt Relish.

250 g gram flour (besan)
1 teaspoon chilli powder (mild, medium or hot, as desired)
1 teaspoon ground turmeric
1 tablespoon coriander seeds, crushed
3 large onions, sliced
6 fresh curry leaves
sunflower oil, for deep-frying
salt

makes about 15

spiced potatoes

This spiced potato dish from Mumbai is terrific when served with Poori (page 84) and Coriander & Mint Chutney (page 88) for a light snack or a Sunday brunch with a difference.

500 g potatoes, peeled and cubed

4 tablespoons sunflower oil

2 teaspoons black mustard seeds

1 teaspoon medium or hot chilli powder, or paprika

4 teaspoons cumin seeds

8–10 fresh curry leaves

2 teaspoons ground cumin

2 teaspoons ground coriander

1 teaspoon ground turmeric

6 tablespoons freshly chopped coriander leaves

freshly squeezed lemon juice, to taste

salt and freshly ground black pepper

serves 4

Cook the potatoes in a pan of salted boiling water until tender.

Heat the sunflower oil in a large, non-stick wok or frying pan. Add the mustard seeds, chilli powder, cumin seeds and curry leaves. Stir-fry for 1–2 minutes, then add the ground cumin, ground coriander, turmeric and potatoes. Season well and stir-fry over high heat for 4–5 minutes.

Stir in the fresh coriander and lemon juice, to taste, and serve with poori and Coriander & Mint Chutney.

saag paneer

Paneer is an Indian cow's milk cheese easily found in Asian greengrocers. Here it is paired with spinach and tomato for a popular Indian dish.

500 g frozen spinach

50 g ghee or butter

2 teaspoons cumin seeds

1 onion, very finely chopped

2 plum tomatoes, finely chopped

2 teaspoons crushed garlic

1 tablespoon finely grated fresh ginger

1 teaspoon chilli powder (mild, medium or hot, as desired)

1 teaspoon ground coriander

250 g paneer, cut into bite-sized pieces

2 tablespoons double cream

2 tablespoons freshly chopped coriander leaves

1 teaspoon freshly squeezed lemon juice

salt and freshly ground black pepper

serves 4

Bring a large saucepan of water to the boil. Add the frozen spinach and bring back to the boil. Cook for 2–3 minutes, then drain thoroughly. Transfer to a food processor and blend until smooth.

Heat the ghee in a large, heavy-based frying pan. Add the cumin seeds and onion and stir-fry for 6–8 minutes over medium/low heat until the onion turns lightly golden. Add the tomatoes, garlic, ginger, chilli powder and ground coriander. Season well. Stir-fry for 2–3 minutes. Add the paneer and cook for 30–40 seconds over high heat. Add the blended spinach and stir-fry for 4–5 minutes. Stir in the cream, fresh coriander and lemon juice.

Punjabi cabbage

Eaten widely in Punjab and northern India, green cabbage is quick to cook and excellent served with any main vegetarian or meat dishes.

Heat the sunflower oil in a large, non-stick wok or frying pan over low heat. Add the shallots, ginger, garlic and chillies and stir-fry for 2–3 minutes, or until the shallots have softened.

Add the cumin seeds, turmeric and coriander seeds and stir-fry for 1 minute.

Turn the heat to high and add the cabbage, tossing well to coat in the spice mixture. Add the curry powder and season well. Cover and cook over medium heat for 10 minutes, stirring occasionally. Stir in the ghee and serve.

3 tablespoons sunflower oil

4 shallots, finely chopped

2 teaspoons finely grated fresh ginger

2 teaspoons crushed garlic

2 green chillies, halved lengthways

2 teaspoons cumin seeds

1 teaspoon ground turmeric

1 teaspoon coriander seeds, crushed

500 g green or white cabbage, shredded

1 tablespoon mild or medium curry powder

1 tablespoon ghee or butter

salt and freshly ground black pepper

serves 4

pulses

Imagine a glorious helping of comfort food – not macaroni cheese, Mum's mashed potatoes or your signature dish of toast, but **chickpea masala (page 70)**, slow-cooked to perfection, or a bowl of red split lentils and rice spiked with warming spices – **kitcheree (page 72)** which evolved into kedgeree as we know it today. There's something about beans, peas and lentils (dal in Indian) which render a dish hearty, wholesome and somehow meaty without the need for any meat. So integral are they to the Indian diet that they deserve a chapter all of their own. By themselves, lentils, chickpeas and kidney beans lack punch, but team them up with the likes of turmeric, cumin, chillies, curry leaves and ginger, and you get a magical **tarka dal (page 69)**. One of my abiding memories from childhood is of our cook crushing and pounding wet and dry spices on a granite grinding stone with a kind of rolling pin. The colours and fragrances produced in this arduous process were unforgettable, and made it a real labour of love. **Spiced aubergine dal (page 73)** benefits from being made a day in advance, and in fact many lentils and beans do need soaking overnight, such as in the **spinach dal (page 69)**, but you can cheat the **red kidney bean curry (page 74)** by using good-quality organic tinned beans instead.

tarka dal

This is the ultimate Indian comfort food. Cooked lentils are given a final seasoning with a spiced oil called 'tarka' to give the dish its distinctive flavour.

250 g dried red split lentils

1 teaspoon ground turmeric

4 ripe tomatoes, roughly chopped

6–8 tablespoons freshly chopped coriander leaves

tarka

4 tablespoons sunflower oil

2 teaspoons black mustard seeds

3 teaspoons cumin seeds

2 garlic cloves, very thinly sliced

2 teaspoons very finely chopped fresh ginger

6–8 fresh curry leaves

1 dried red chilli

2 teaspoons ground cumin

2 teaspoons ground coriander

salt and freshly ground black pepper

serves 4

Rinse the lentils until the water runs clear. Place in a heavy-based saucepan with 1 litre water. Bring to the boil over high heat, skimming off any scum that rises to the surface. Lower the heat and cook for 20–25 minutes. Remove from the heat and using a hand-held blender or whisk, blend until smooth. Return to the heat and stir in the turmeric and tomatoes. Bring to the boil, season and stir in the coriander. To make the tarka, heat the sunflower oil in a frying pan. Add all the ingredients and stir-fry for 1–2 minutes. Stir into the dal.

spinach dal

Also known as 'kali dal' (which means whole black lentils) this simple yet scrumptious dish is a staple food across India. Serve with bread and pickles.

120 g dried black lentils

3 tablespoons butter

1 onion, finely chopped

3 garlic cloves, crushed

2 teaspoons finely grated fresh ginger

2 green chillies, halved lengthways

1 teaspoon ground turmeric

1 teaspoon paprika

1 tablespoon ground coriander

1 tablespoon ground cumin

200 g tinned red kidney beans, drained and rinsed

200 g baby leaf spinach

a large handful of fresh coriander leaves, chopped

150 ml double cream

serves 4

Rinse the lentils. Drain, place in a deep bowl and cover with cold water. Leave to soak for 10–12 hours. Rinse the lentils, then place in a saucepan with 500 ml boiling water. Bring to the boil, reduce the heat and simmer for 35–40 minutes, or until tender. Drain and set aside. Melt the butter in a saucepan and stir-fry the onion, garlic, ginger and chillies for 5–6 minutes, then add the turmeric, paprika, ground coriander, cumin, kidney beans and lentils. Add 500 ml water and bring to the boil. Reduce the heat and stir in the spinach. Cook gently for 10–15 minutes, stirring often. Stir in the coriander and cream.

chickpea masala

This street food of spiced chickpeas is served at little food stalls in the bazaars and markets all over India. Usually eaten with Poori (page 84), it makes a great accompaniment to any Indian meal.

Heat the sunflower oil in a large, heavy-based frying pan over medium heat and add the garlic, ginger, onion and chillies. Stir-fry for 6–8 minutes, or until the onion is lightly golden. Add the chilli powder, cumin, ground coriander, yoghurt and garam masala and stir-fry for 1–2 minutes.

Stir in 500 ml water and bring to the boil. Add the tamarind paste, curry powder and chickpeas and bring back to the boil. Reduce the heat to low and simmer gently for 30–40 minutes, stirring occasionally, or until the liquid has reduced, coating the chickpeas in a dark, rich sauce.

Serve in little bowls drizzled with a little whisked yoghurt, garnished with chopped coriander and chilli powder, and with lemon wedges on the side.

4 tablespoons sunflower oil

4 garlic cloves, crushed

2 teaspoons finely grated fresh ginger

1 large onion, coarsely grated

1–2 green chillies, thinly sliced

1 teaspoon hot chilli powder, plus extra to garnish

1 tablespoon ground cumin

1 tablespoon ground coriander

3 tablespoons natural yoghurt, plus extra, whisked, to drizzle

2 teaspoons garam masala

2 teaspoons tamarind paste

2 teaspoons medium curry powder

two 400-g tins chickpeas, drained and rinsed

freshly chopped coriander leaves, to garnish

lemon wedges, to serve

serves 4

kitcheree

This dish began life as a simple combination of lentils cooked with rice and a few spices. In the British Raj, it was taken to a different level with the addition of smoked fish and boiled eggs and called kedgeree. Serve with pickles, if you like.

Rinse the lentils and rice until the water runs clear. Drain thoroughly.

Heat the sunflower oil in a heavy-based saucepan and add the onion. Stir-fry for 6–8 minutes over medium heat, then add the turmeric, cumin seeds, chilli, cinnamon, cloves and cardamom pods. Continue to stir-fry for 2–3 minutes, then add the rice and lentils. Stir-fry for 2–3 minutes, then add the stock and coriander. Season well and bring to the boil. Reduce the heat to low, cover tightly and cook for 10 minutes. Remove from the heat and leave to stand undisturbed for another 10 minutes.

Transfer to a serving dish and serve with yoghurt and pickles on the side.

125 g dried red split lentils

225 g basmati rice

3 tablespoons sunflower oil

1 onion, finely chopped

1 teaspoon ground turmeric

1 tablespoon cumin seeds

1 dried red chilli

1 cinnamon stick

3 cloves

3 cardamom pods, lightly bruised

500 ml vegetable stock

8 tablespoons freshly chopped coriander leaves

salt and freshly ground black pepper

natural yoghurt, to serve

serves 4

spiced aubergine dal

Dals can be made from many different varieties of lentils. Here we use the yellow split lentils which require no soaking and cook quickly. It benefits from being made a day in advance, which gives the flavours time to mingle and mellow. Serve with steamed basmati rice or bread.

Heat the sunflower oil in a saucepan over high heat. Add the onions and stir-fry for 6–8 minutes, until they start to become golden. Reduce the heat and stir in the garlic, ginger, cumin seeds, mustard seeds and curry powder. Stir-fry for 1–2 minutes, then add the lentils and 600 ml water. Bring to the boil, add the aubergine and cherry tomatoes and reduce the heat to low. Cover and simmer gently for 25–30 minutes, stirring occasionally, until the dal is thick and the lentils are tender.

Season well with salt and stir in the coriander. Serve with steamed basmati rice or bread.

3 tablespoons sunflower oil

2 onions, finely chopped

4 garlic cloves, finely chopped

1 teaspoon finely grated fresh ginger

1 tablespoon cumin seeds

1 tablespoon black mustard seeds

2 tablespoons curry powder
(mild, medium or hot, as desired)

175 g dried yellow split lentils

1 aubergine, cut into bite-sized pieces

8 cherry tomatoes

8 tablespoons freshly chopped coriander leaves

salt

serves 4

red kidney bean curry

Dried red kidney beans are turned into the perfect comfort food, in this lightly spiced curry. If pushed for time, you can use very good-quality organic tinned red kidney beans instead.

Put the red kidney beans in a large saucepan, cover with cold water and leave to soak overnight.

Drain the soaked beans and return to the saucepan with double the amount of water. Bring to the boil, then keep boiling for 15 minutes. Reduce the heat to medium/low and simmer gently for 1 hour, or until the beans are tender. Drain, reserving the cooking liquid.

Heat the butter and sunflower oil in a large, heavy-based saucepan and add the onion, cinnamon, bay leaves, garlic and ginger and stir-fry for 4–5 minutes. Stir in the turmeric, ground coriander, cumin, garam masala and chillies.

Add the beans, tomato purée and enough of the reserved cooking liquid to make a thick sauce. Bring to the boil and cook for 4–5 minutes, stirring often.

Season well, drizzle with whisked yoghurt, if desired, and garnish with fresh coriander.

250 g dried red kidney beans
1 tablespoon butter
2 tablespoons sunflower oil
1 onion, finely chopped
a 5-cm piece of cinnamon stick or cassia bark
2 dried bay leaves
3 garlic cloves, crushed
2 teaspoons finely grated fresh ginger
½ teaspoon ground turmeric
1 teaspoon ground coriander
2 teaspoons ground cumin
1 teaspoon garam masala
2 dried red chillies
4 tablespoons tomato purée
salt and freshly ground black pepper
whisked yoghurt, to drizzle (optional)
freshly chopped coriander leaves, to serve

serves 4

rice & breads

One of the most irresistible things about curry is the sauce which often accompanies it, so it follows that you will need something on the side for scooping or soaking up. Punchy or barely there, light as air or densely satisfying – rice and breads have everything to offer. In fact, even the simplest curry simply wouldn't be right without **lemon** or **coconut rice (both page 78)** or fluffy **naan (page 85)** on the side. So moreish are the flatbreads, for example, that it is common in India to snack on a freshly cooked **saag roti (page 84)** with a generous dollop of chutney. I can't recommend it enough. Delicate, puffed-up **poori (page 84)** complement spicy potatoes and fish curries beautifully. And **morel mushroom pulao (page 82)** is a rice dish with a difference – smoky morsels of morels amidst cinnamon- and cardamom-scented basmati. Meanwhile, **lamb biryani (page 81)** is usually reserved as a special-occasion dish since it takes a while to cook. During festivals such as Diwali, huge pots of biryani are placed over coals along the street and their lids are carefully sealed in place with a flour-and-water mixture to ensure that no flavours or heat are lost during cooking, resulting in the tenderest chunks of lamb and fluffiest rice. An entire one-pot meal, lovingly prepared and left to steam to a meltingly soft consistency.

lemon rice

A typical southern Indian favourite, this citrussy **rice dish is a perfect accompaniment to plain grilled fish or chicken, or steamed vegetables.**

225 g basmati rice
1 tablespoon light olive oil
12–14 fresh curry leaves
1 dried red chilli
2 cassia barks or cinnamon sticks
2–3 cloves
4–6 cardamom pods, bruised
2 teaspoons cumin seeds
¼ teaspoon ground turmeric
freshly squeezed juice of 1 large lemon
450 ml boiling water
salt and freshly ground black pepper

serves 4

Rinse the rice until the water runs clear. Drain thoroughly and set aside.

Heat the olive oil in a non-stick saucepan and add the curry leaves, chilli, cassia, cloves, cardamom pods, cumin seeds and turmeric. Stir-fry for 20–30 seconds, then add the rice. Stir-fry for 2 minutes, then add the lemon juice and boiling water. Season well and bring to the boil. Cover the pan tightly, reduce the heat to low and cook for 10–12 minutes.

Leave to stand undisturbed for 10 minutes. Fluff up the rice with a fork and season.

coconut rice

This aromatic and mildly flavoured rice dish acts as a perfect foil to any spicy curry.

225 g basmati rice
2 tablespoons sunflower oil
2 teaspoons black mustard seeds
2 teaspoons cumin seeds
2 dried red chillies
10 fresh curry leaves
500 ml hot water
4 tablespoons coconut cream
2 tablespoons freshly grated coconut, to garnish

serves 4

Rinse the rice until the water runs clear. Transfer to a bowl, cover with cold water and leave to soak for 15 minutes. Drain thoroughly.

Heat the sunflower oil in a heavy-based saucepan and add the mustard seeds, cumin seeds, chillies and curry leaves. Stir-fry for 30 seconds, then add the hot water and coconut cream. Stir well and bring to the boil. Reduce the heat to low, cover tightly and cook for 10 minutes.

Leave to stand undisturbed for 10 minutes. Fluff up the rice with a fork and scatter over the grated coconut.

lamb biryani

This one-pot rice and lamb preparation was traditionally cooked during royal festival days. It can be made with chicken, seafood or vegetables too. Serve with Onion, Cucumber & Tomato Relish or Cucumber & Yoghurt Relish (both page 88) for maximum enjoyment!

To make the marinade, combine the garlic, ginger, yoghurt and coriander in a glass bowl. Add the lamb and rub the marinade into the lamb pieces. Cover and marinate in the fridge for 4–6 hours.

Heat the sunflower oil in a heavy-based pan, add the onion and cook for 12–15 minutes, until lightly golden. Add the marinated lamb and cook over high heat for 15 minutes, stirring often. Stir in the ground coriander, cumin, chilli powder, turmeric and tinned tomatoes, season well and bring to the boil. Reduce the heat to low and simmer gently for 30 minutes, or until the lamb is tender and most of the liquid has been absorbed. Set aside.

Prepare the rice. Heat the sunflower oil in a heavy-based pan. Add the cumin seeds, onion, cloves, peppercorns, cardamom pods and cinnamon and stir-fry for 6–8 minutes. Add the rice and stir-fry for 2 minutes. Pour in 400 ml water and bring to the boil. Cover and simmer gently for 6–7 minutes. Set aside. Mix the saffron and milk and set aside.

Preheat the oven to 180°C (350°F) Gas 4.

Put a thin layer of the meat mixture in the casserole and cover with half the rice. Drizzle over half the saffron mixture. Top with the remaining lamb mixture and cover with the remaining rice. Drizzle over the remaining saffron mixture, cover the dish with foil, then cover with the lid. Bake in the preheated oven for 30 minutes. Remove from the oven and leave to rest, still covered, for 30 minutes before serving.

500 g boned leg of lamb, cut into bite-sized pieces

4 tablespoons sunflower oil

1 onion, finely chopped

1 tablespoon ground coriander

1 teaspoon ground cumin

1 teaspoon mild or medium chilli powder

1 teaspoon ground turmeric

225 g tinned chopped tomatoes

marinade

4 garlic cloves, crushed

1 teaspoon finely grated fresh ginger

150 ml natural yoghurt

6 tablespoons freshly chopped coriander leaves

rice

4 tablespoons sunflower oil

2 teaspoons cumin seeds

1 onion, thinly sliced

6 cloves

10 black peppercorns

4 cardamom pods

1 cinnamon stick

225 g basmati rice

1 teaspoon saffron threads

3 tablespoons warm milk

an ovenproof casserole with a tight-fitting lid, lightly buttered

serves 4

morel mushroom pulao

'Gucchi' is the name for the wild morel mushrooms found in the forests of Kashmir. They are extremely expensive to buy fresh, so smoky dried morels are used in this rich rice dish.

Put the mushrooms in a glass bowl with the boiling water. Cover and leave to stand for 20–30 minutes, or until the mushrooms have re-hydrated and are soft. Strain the mushrooms through a fine sieve, reserving the liquid.

Rinse the rice until the water runs clear. Transfer to a bowl, cover with cold water and leave to soak for 20 minutes. Drain thoroughly.

Heat the sunflower oil in a heavy-based saucepan and add the cinnamon, cumin seeds, cloves, cardamom pods, peppercorns and dried onions. Stir-fry for 2–3 minutes, then add the drained mushrooms and the peas. Stir-fry for 2–3 minutes, then add the rice. Pour in the reserved mushroom liquid and season well. Bring to the boil, cover tightly and reduce the heat to low. Cook for 8–10 minutes, then remove from the heat and leave to stand, covered, for 10 minutes. Fluff up the rice with a fork before serving.

30 g dried morel mushrooms
600 ml boiling water
275 g basmati rice
4 tablespoons sunflower oil
1 cinnamon stick
2 teaspoons cumin seeds
2 cloves
4 cardamom pods, lightly bruised
8 black peppercorns
4 tablespoons dried onions
200 g frozen peas
salt and freshly ground black pepper

serves 4

poori

These deep-fried wholemeal breads are usually eaten with spicy potatoes or seafood curries. They are sometimes also eaten with a sweet yoghurt dessert called 'shrikand'.

250 g wholemeal flour
a pinch of salt
2 tablespoons ghee, melted
sunflower oil, for deep-frying

makes 20

Combine the flour and salt in a large bowl. Add the ghee and a little cold water (60–80 ml) to make a stiff dough. Cover with a damp cloth and refrigerate for 30 minutes.

Divide the dough into 20 portions and shape each one into a ball. Flatten them with the palm of your hand, then roll out into a 10-cm disc.

Fill a large wok one-third full with sunflower oil and heat over moderate heat to 180°C or until a piece of bread dropped in sizzles and browns within 10 seconds. Carefully drop in the pooris in batches and deep-fry for 1–2 minutes on each side, or until puffed up and golden. Remove with a slotted spoon and drain on kitchen paper. Eat immediately.

saag roti

These flatbreads are made with chapatti flour (atta), available from Asian supermarkets. If you can't find it, use an equal mix of wholemeal and plain flour.

100 g courgettes, coarsely grated
100 g baby spinach leaves, roughly chopped
500 g chapatti flour (atta), plus extra to dust
a large pinch of salt
1 tablespoon cumin seeds, lightly toasted in a dry frying pan
1 red chilli, deseeded and finely chopped
4 tablespoons ghee or melted butter
sunflower oil, for brushing

makes 20

Put the grated courgettes in a sieve and squeeze out as much liquid as you can. Put the flesh in a mixing bowl. Blanch the spinach in a large saucepan of boiling water until just wilted, drain thoroughly and squeeze out as much liquid as you can. Add the spinach to the courgettes.

Sift the flour into a bowl with the salt. Stir in the cumin seeds, chilli, and courgette and spinach mixture. Stir in the ghee along with 250 ml lukewarm water. Mix to form a soft, pliable dough, then turn out on to a floured surface and knead for 4–5 minutes. Transfer to an oiled bowl, cover and leave to rest for 30 minutes.

Divide the dough into 20 pieces. Roll out each piece to a 12-cm disc about 5 mm thick. Heat a large, heavy-based frying pan until hot, lightly brush with oil and cook one at a time for 1–2 minutes on each side, until lightly blistered and cooked through. Cover with a tea towel and keep warm while you cook the rest. Serve with Tarka Dal and any curry.

naan

Naan is one of the most popular leavened breads from India, traditionally cooked in a tandoori or clay oven. Luckily it works just as well under a grill.

450 g self-raising flour
2 teaspoons sugar
1 teaspoon salt
1 teaspoon baking powder
8 tablespoons melted butter or ghee, plus extra for brushing
250 ml milk, warmed
2 tablespoons nigella seeds

makes 8

Sift the flour, sugar, salt and baking powder into a large bowl. Add the melted butter and rub into the flour mixture with your fingers. Gradually add the warm milk and mix until you get a soft dough. Transfer to a lightly floured surface and knead for 6–8 minutes, or until smooth. Put back in the bowl, cover with clingfilm and leave to rest for 20–25 minutes.

Divide the mixture into 8 pieces and flatten each one slightly. Cover with a tea towel and leave to rest for 10–15 minutes.

Put the dough on a lightly floured surface and roll each piece into a 23-cm disc. Brush the tops of the breads with melted butter and sprinkle over the nigella seeds. Put the breads on a lightly oiled grill rack and cook in batches, under a medium/high grill for 1–2 minutes on each side, or until puffed up and lightly brown in spots. Wrap in a tea towel and keep warm while you cook the rest. Serve warm with any curry.

extras

Chutney, relish and pickles – all loyal curry companions and all essential in making a meal complete. To temper, enrich or pep up, these extras are apt to fulfil any role. Even if all you want is to fill your plate with more finger-licking morsels, then **samosas (page 91)** are perfect extras. What's more, a bowl of **coriander & mint chutney**, **cucumber & yoghurt relish** or **onion, cucumber & tomato relish (all page 88)** is so tempting that it's as good served as a dip when you've got the munchies, as it is as a bona fide accompaniment to a full-blown curry. In India, every household makes its own chutney and relish and stores them – it goes without saying that a home-made **mango chutney** or **carrot pickle (both page 93)** beats anything you can buy from a shop so it's worth putting some jars together one weekend when you have an hour to spare. For a taste of the Tropics, nothing beats a **coconut chutney (page 92)** – snowy white and speckled with black mustard seeds and yellow split lentils. And let's not forget the ever-popular extras: poppadoms. Uncooked poppadoms are easy to find in supermarkets now, and just need to be fried or even popped in the microwave. But if you want to make more of them, try my **prawn & poppadom rolls (page 90)**. There's no excuse not to bring a little of the inimitable Indian flair for flavour combinations into your home.

onion, cucumber & tomato relish

This is a finely chopped salad called 'kachumber' and a common accompaniment in Indian meals. It is also great as a relish with poppadoms and bread.

1 red onion, finely chopped
1 cucumber, finely chopped
4 ripe tomatoes, finely chopped
a small handful of fresh coriander leaves, finely chopped
1 red chilli, deseeded and finely chopped (optional)
freshly squeezed juice of 1 large lemon
50 g roasted peanuts, roughly chopped

serves 4

Put the onion, cucumber, tomatoes, coriander and chilli, if using, in a bowl and pour over the lemon juice. Season well, cover and leave to stand for 10–15 minutes.

Before serving, stir well to mix and sprinkle over the chopped peanuts. This will keep in the fridge for up to 3 days.

coriander & mint chutney

Quick and easy to prepare, this aromatic, fresh-tasting relish is great as a dip for snacks or to serve alongside grilled meat, chicken or fish.

200 g fresh coriander leaves, finely chopped
200 g fresh mint leaves, finely chopped
freshly squeezed juice of 2 limes
2 green chillies, deseeded and chopped
1 tablespoon finely grated fresh ginger
100 g thick, Greek-style yoghurt
1 teaspoon ground cumin
1 teaspoon mild chilli powder
1 teaspoon sugar
sea salt

makes about 400 ml

Put the coriander, mint, lime juice, chillies, ginger, yoghurt, cumin, chilli powder and sugar in a small food processor and blitz until smooth (you might need to add a couple of tablespoons of water).

Season with sea salt and transfer to a bowl. Cover and chill until ready to use. This will keep in the fridge for up to 3 days.

cucumber & yoghurt relish

'Raita' is a cool, yoghurt-based relish which can be made from a variety of ingredients. This one is made with cucumber and mint – ideal for tempering a spicy meal.

1 small cucumber (approximately 15 cm), peeled and coarsely grated
350 g natural yoghurt, whisked
5 tablespoons freshly chopped mint leaves
1–2 teaspoons cumin seeds, lightly toasted in a dry frying pan
salt and freshly ground black pepper
mild or medium chilli powder, to sprinkle (optional)

serves 4

Put the grated cucumber in a sieve and squeeze out as much liquid as you can. Transfer to a bowl with the yoghurt and mint. Season well and chill until ready to serve. Sprinkle over the cumin seeds and chilli powder, if using, just before serving. This will keep in the fridge for up to 3 days.

prawn & poppadom rolls

Poppadoms are very thin dried discs made from a variety of different lentils. They are usually roasted or fried and served as a snack or a crispy accompaniment to a meal. Here they are stuffed with a spicy prawn mixture and deep-fried. Uncooked poppadoms can now easily be found in most supermarkets. Serve with mixed, dressed salad leaves, if you like.

Heat the sunflower oil in a large frying pan and add the onion. Cook over gentle heat for 6–8 minutes or until softened. Add the garlic, ginger, cumin seeds and curry powder and stir-fry for 1–2 minutes.

Add the prawns and potatoes and stir well to mix. Season and stir in the chopped coriander and lime juice. Remove from the heat and set aside to cool.

Put the flour in a small bowl and stir in enough cold water to make a smooth, thick paste.

Soak the uncooked poppadoms in warm water for 3–4 minutes, or until just softened. Drain well, pat dry with kitchen paper and put on a clean surface.

Spoon one-eighth of the prawn mixture on to one side of a poppadom. Carefully roll it up, folding in the sides to enclose the filling. Apply a little flour paste around the edges to seal. Repeat with the remaining prawn mixture and poppadoms to make the remaining rolls.

Fill a large saucepan one-third full with vegetable oil and heat to 160°C or until a piece of bread dropped in sizzles and lightly browns within 10 seconds. Carefully lower the stuffed rolls into the hot oil in batches and deep-fry for 2 minutes, or until golden and crisp. Drain thoroughly on kitchen paper and serve with mixed, dressed salad leaves, if desired.

1 tablespoon sunflower oil

1 onion, finely chopped

1 teaspoon crushed garlic

1 teaspoon finely grated fresh ginger

2 teaspoons cumin seeds

1 tablespoon medium curry powder

150 g uncooked tiger prawns, shelled, deveined and roughly chopped

150 g peeled and cooked potatoes, roughly chopped

4 tablespoons freshly chopped coriander leaves

freshly squeezed juice of ½ lime

2 tablespoons plain flour

8 medium-sized, uncooked poppadoms

vegetable oil, for deep-frying

salt and freshly ground black pepper

serves 4

samosas

These popular golden stuffed parcels can be filled with a variety of vegetable or meat mixtures. Here they are simply stuffed with spiced minced chicken.

Heat the sunflower oil in a frying pan. Add the chicken, onion and curry powder. Season and cook for about 10 minutes, uncovered, until the chicken is just cooked and the juices have evaporated from the pan. Add the potato and peas and mix well. Remove the pan from the heat and stir in the chopped coriander and mint. Leave to cool.

Lay the filo pastry out on a clean board and cut in half lengthways, then in half once more widthways, so that you have 4 rectangles from each whole sheet. Cover all the pieces of filo with a barely damp tea towel to prevent them from drying out. Take one piece of filo and lay it widthways in front of you. Pile a dessertspoon of the chicken mixture on to the end closest to you. Fold the filo over the filling to form a triangle and continue to fold and enclose the filling until you have a triangular parcel. Brush the finishing edge with a little of the beaten egg to seal, then place on a baking tray. Glaze the finished samosa all over with beaten egg and repeat the process until you have 20 samosas. These can be prepared earlier in the day up to this point and chilled in the fridge.

When ready to bake the samosas, preheat the oven to 220°C (425°F) Gas 7.

Bake the samosas in the preheated oven for 10–12 minutes, until golden brown in colour.

2 tablespoons sunflower oil

300 g minced chicken

1 onion, chopped

1 tablespoon medium curry powder

50 g peeled and cooked potato, diced

50 g frozen peas

4 tablespoons freshly chopped coriander leaves

4 tablespoons freshly chopped mint leaves

5 sheets of filo pastry, each 25 x 50 cm

1 egg, beaten

salt and freshly ground black pepper

makes 20

coconut chutney

This is made with freshly grated coconut, however you could use about 150 g desiccated coconut instead – just soak in hot water for 20–30 minutes, then drain well and use as below.

2 teaspoons dried yellow split lentils
200 g freshly grated coconut
2 green chillies, deseeded and finely chopped
1 teaspoon sea salt
2 tablespoons sunflower oil
2 teaspoons black mustard seeds
6–8 fresh curry leaves
1 dried red chilli
1 teaspoon tamarind paste

serves 4

Rinse the lentils until the water runs clear. Drain, place in a deep bowl and cover with cold water. Leave to soak for 2–3 hours. Rinse the lentils, drain and set aside.

Put the coconut, green chillies and salt in a food processor and blend to a fine paste (you might need to add a couple of tablespoons of water). Transfer to a bowl.

Heat the sunflower oil in a small frying pan and add the mustard seeds and reserved lentils. Cook over gentle heat and when the mustard seeds start to pop, add the curry leaves and dried chilli and stir-fry for 1 minute.

Add the spice paste and tamarind paste to the pan, stir well to mix, and transfer to a bowl.

mango chutney

This lightly spiced, sweet chutney provides a lovely contrast to a spicy meal and is perhaps one of the best known and loved Indian chutneys.

1 tablespoon sunflower oil

1 teaspoon finely grated fresh ginger

2 garlic cloves, crushed

5 cloves

1 star anise

2 cassia barks or cinnamon sticks

5 black peppercorns

1–2 tablespoons nigella seeds

½ teaspoon mild or medium chilli powder

800 g ripe but firm mango flesh, roughly chopped

400 ml white wine vinegar

270 g caster sugar

sea salt

1–3 sterilized jam jars (see page 4)

makes about 500 ml

Heat the sunflower oil in a saucepan over medium heat. Add the ginger, garlic, cloves, star anise, cassia, peppercorns, nigella seeds and chilli powder and stir-fry for 1–2 minutes. Add the mango, vinegar and sugar and bring to the boil. Reduce the heat to low and cook for 45 minutes, or until the mixture is jam-like.

Season with sea salt to taste and pour into the hot sterilized jars. Seal and leave to cool before storing in the fridge for up to 2 months.

carrot pickle

Crunchy, spicy and full of zing, this carrot pickle will perk up even the simplest meal.

500 g carrots, cut into 5-cm batons

200 g small red shallots, peeled

6–8 green chillies

150 ml white wine vinegar

½ teaspoon ground turmeric

sea salt

pickling paste

150 ml white wine vinegar

4 garlic cloves, crushed

2 teaspoons finely grated fresh ginger

1 tablespoon black mustard seeds

2 teaspoons mild or medium chilli powder

1 tablespoon sugar

1–3 sterilized jam jars (see page 4)

makes about 800 ml

Put the carrots, shallots, chillies, vinegar and turmeric in a saucepan with 300 ml water and season with sea salt. Bring to the boil and cook for 3–4 minutes. Drain and set aside.

To make the pickling paste, put the vinegar, garlic, ginger, mustard seeds, chilli powder and sugar in a small food processor and blend until fairly smooth. Season with sea salt and transfer to a mixing bowl. Add the drained vegetable mixture and toss to coat evenly. Transfer to the hot sterilized jars. Seal and store in a cool, dark place for 2 weeks before eating. Store in the fridge after opening and eat within 2 months.

websites & mail order

Fudco
www.alpertonict.com/Riquene/index.html
184 Ealing Road
Wembley
Middlesex HA0 4QP
Tel: 020 8902 4820
*Good local shop and website stocking
spices, seeds, home-made pickles, masalas,
herbs and more.*

John Lewis
www.johnlewis.com
Tel: 08456 049 049
*Good assortment of cookware, including
frying pans and woks, spice grinders and
pestles and mortars.*

Natco
www.natco-online.com
*Fantastic range of Indian food, spices and
cooking ingredients, including gram and
chapatti flour, lentils and beans, white
poppy seeds, jaggery and ghee.*

Peppers by Post
www.peppersbypost.biz
Sea Spring Farm
West Bexington
Dorchester
Dorset DT2 9DD
Tel: 01308 897766
*Family business based in Dorset which
grows many varieties of chillies, including
hot Thai and chilli plants to grow at home.*

Seasoned Pioneers
www.seasonedpioneers.com
Tel: 0800 0682348
*Authentic spices, chillies, herbs, specialist
seasonings and spice blends from all
around the world.*

The Spice of Life
www.thespiceoflife.co.uk
Dried herbs and spices for curry fans.

Spices of India
www.spicesofindia.co.uk
Tel: 01202 873298
*A huge range Indian spices, sweet,
ingredients and tableware, such as
stainless steel cookware designed to be
used on the hob or in the oven and
transferred straight to the table. Also sell
Thai ingredients (kaffir lime leaves, Thai
curry paste, etc).*

The Spice Shop
www.thespiceshop.co.uk
1 Blenheim Crescent
London W11 2EE
Tel: 020 7221 4448
*An oasis of spices from all over the world
in London's Portobello Market.*

index